TEMPLE NEWSAM
PAINTINGS

LEEDS MUSEUMS & GALLERIES

Front cover: Antonio Marini, *Seascape with Shipwreck*
(detail of no 23)

Inside front cover: Antonio Joli, *View on the Tiber*
(detail of no 25)

Title page: James Chapman, *A Prospect of Temple Newsam c1750*

Inside back cover: Antonio Joli, *Architectural Fantasy*
(detail of no 26)

Back cover: Balthasar van der Ast, *Floral Studies with Beaker,
Grasshopper and Seashells*

ISBN 0-901 981-67-2

Published 2000 by Leeds Museums and Galleries,
c/o The Town Hall, The Headrow, Leeds LS1 3AD

Text by James Lomax
Designed by Farmer Design Associates, Huddersfield
Printed by Polestar Corporate Print Ltd, Bradford

Fig. 1 The Picture Gallery,
Temple Newsam c1874

Introduction

Temple Newsam, the vast Tudor-Jacobean mansion lying in 917 acres of parkland four miles to the east of Leeds, is justly famous as one of the great historic houses of England. It has also become celebrated for the collections of decorative arts, especially furniture, silver, ceramics, textiles and wallpapers, which have been built up since 1922 when the estate was bought from the Hon Edward Wood (later Earl of Halifax) by the city of Leeds and developed as a country house museum. The collection of fine art is less well-known and so this small book presents a selection of some of the most interesting paintings.

Since about 1979 the policy of Leeds Art Galleries (now Leeds Museums and Galleries) has been to display all its Old Master and British paintings dating from before 1840 at Temple Newsam, while later 19TH and 20TH century art is shown at the City Art Gallery. The Gascoigne family paintings and some Impressionists are exhibited at Lotherton Hall, Aberford. This policy works extraordinarily well in bringing together both the fine and decorative arts to be shown in the context of the historic settings for which many of them were originally created.

Today there are approximately 400 paintings hanging at Temple Newsam nearly all on display in the 33 rooms normally open to the public (this figure compares with 79 in 1688, 129 in c1721, 188 in c1862 and 209 in 1902). Of these about half are indigenous to the house, having been assembled over 300 years by the Ingram family and their successors. The rest have joined the collection from other sources by gift, bequest and purchase.

By far the most significant moment in the history of the collection came when Lord Halifax returned 85 'heirloom' paintings to the house in 1948. Despite a number of the 'star pieces' having been sold or retained by the family after 1922, Lord Halifax's act remains by far the most generous gift of an aristocratic collection to a local authority in the history of museum patronage in this country. The major part of the gift were family portraits: since many of these are illustrated in the house guidebook and are best considered in the context of the history of the house, they are not included here. A small number of pictures collected by the Wood family of Hickleton and Garrowby also joined the Temple Newsam collection with this gift (nos 22, 31 and 39).

The mansion built by Thomas Lord Darcy c1500 and given to Lord and Lady Lennox by Henry VIII in 1545 was sparsely furnished

3

with pictures: an inventory of 1565 reveals only nine portraits of family and royalty in the Great Chamber. It was Sir Arthur Ingram's purchase of the property in 1622 and his subsequent rebuilding and lavish furnishing campaign which gave the house its first true collection. Apart from his own resplendent portrait by George Geldorp none of his scriptural or mythological pictures by the Flemish and Italian masters have survived, although *Eliezir and Rebecca at the Well* (no 6) may well have come to Temple Newsam at about this time. All that remains today from this period is the extraordinary series of *Prophets* and *The Last Supper* (after Titian) by John Carleton which clad the Laudian chapel.

In 1688 an inventory was compiled identifying 79 paintings: predictably the majority were portraits, but it also included 'two dozen small Dutch pictures' (valued at £1-10-00), and an unusual *St Francis* (school of Francesco Herrera, once attributed to van Dyck) recently returned to Temple Newsam. By 1702 a number of sporting pictures and still lives had arrived, some of them bought through the artist-dealer Leonard Knyff with whom Lady Irwin kept a lively correspondence. But the collection was considerably enhanced as a result of the Grand Tour of Edward, fourth Viscount Irwin (the family having acquired the title at the Restoration). The story of his acquisition of the Marini paintings is told in the notes to no 23; the identity of the artist responsible for this series was soon lost and for nearly two hundred years they appeared in the inventories under the names of 'Borgognone' or 'Ricci'; their re-attribution to Marini and the recent return of the artist's *Self Portrait* (no 24), which must also have arrived at Temple Newsam in 1709, has been extremely welcome.

The picture collection survived the family's reversals following the South Sea Bubble in 1720. Although the property was heavily mortgaged Henry, seventh Viscount Irwin created the spectacular new Picture Gallery in place of Sir Arthur Ingram's Long Gallery, extending most of the length of the first floor of the north wing. Here he hung the cream of the collection in an extraordinarily interesting arrangement. On the north wall, with its six window piers, were a series of full length portraits of royalist heroes of the Civil War centering on a pair of William and Mary which had been personal gifts of the monarch in 1700; this scheme was intended to display the family's consistant loyalty to the Crown (emphasised even more strongly with the plaster medallions of the Hanoverian royal family in the ceiling); below these strong 'political' images were groups of small cabinet pictures easily seen at eye level. For the Kentian overmantels Henry ordered two paintings from Antonio Joli (nos 25 and 26). On the opposite wall hung the full length portraits of his father by Knyff, his brother and sister-in-law Lady Anne Howard by Richardson, and his own portrait with his wife by Mercier. Mercier was a favoured artist with this family in their reduced circumstances at this time (see no 35). Below these, and on the shorter walls, hung the Marinis and other pictures acquired by Edward, fourth Viscount Irwin on his Grand Tour (see also no 15). With its green flock wallpaper and the accompanying gilt furniture the room must have been a magnificent sight when complete in 1746. It was restored as closely as possible to its appearance at this date in 1996 and remarkably it was possible to return over half of the paintings described in an inventory of 1750 to their original locations on the walls.

In 1758 the marriage of Charles, ninth Viscount Irwin to Frances Shepheard, the heiress and natural daughter of a great financier, brought stability to the family and an opportunity to continue picture collecting as never before. Both husband and wife were passionate collectors of real discrimination. Arthur Young described the collection in c1769 as 'not only capital, but very numerous'. During these years they acquired pictures by Rubens, Titian, Claude, Rembrandt and many others; most are now dispersed. Among contemporary British artists they were particularly loyal clients of Sir Joshua Reynolds and Benjamin Wilson.

An inventory compiled in 1808 by Thomas Chippendale the Younger on the death of Lady Irwin shows that the arrangement of the paintings in the Picture Gallery had changed

Author's note

Selected references only are given to the provenance, literature and exhibition history of each of the paintings discussed here. Further information can be found in the following:

Leeds Arts Calendar (118 numbers 1947-95, index contained in nos 117-8, 1996-7)

David Connell, unpublished PhD thesis, *The Collection of Paintings made by the Ingram Family at Temple Newsam from the Seventeenth to the Nineteenth Century*, University of Leeds, Fine Art Department 1992

Hugh Honour, *Catalogue of Paintings: Part I – Works by Artists born before 1800* (1954)

Miranda Strickland-Constable, *Leeds City Art Gallery: A Selection of the Paintings Sculpture Watercolours and Prints* (c1978)

Alexander Robertson, *Leeds City Art Galleries Concise Catalogue: Paintings Sculpture Watercolours Prints* (1976, 1982, and 1997)

OVERLEAF

Fig.2 Portrait of a Man by Titian (Halifax Collection, on loan to the National Gallery, London)

Fig.3 The Holy Family with St John the Baptist by Sir Peter Paul Rubens

Fig.4 Rocky Landscape with a Hermit and a Lay Brother by Pier Francesco Mola (promised bequest of Sir Denis Mahan, on loan to Temple Newsam)

considerably since 1750 although the basic scheme remained right up to 1922. Lady Hertford, the close companion of George IV while Regent and Prince of Wales, who then inherited the house from her mother, made important alterations to the interiors and additions to the furnishings but otherwise left the paintings collection much as she had found it. It remained for the Hon Emily Meynell Ingram, for 33 years the childless and widowed chatelaine of Temple Newsam after the death of her husband in 1871, to complete its history: her enthusiasm was for antiquarian subjects to enhance the historic character of the house (no 5), as well as for landscapes by the Linnells and portraits by the Richmonds. Various critics including Waagen, Augustus Hare, and correspondents in *The Magazine of Art* and *The Athenaeum* were unanimous in their praise of the collection. Titian's *Portrait of a Man* (fig 2) was invariably chosen as the single most beautiful painting.

The dispersal of the collection in 1922 either by sale, or to other properties of the Wood family, left the house nearly empty although a few pictures remained on loan. It was the merger of Temple Newsam with the Art Gallery under the Directorship of Philip Hendy in 1937 which transformed its fortunes. The potential of the house to become a great museum of fine and decorative arts became apparent, above all with the loan exhibition of *Pictures and Furniture from Yorkshire Houses* (1938), many of whose exhibits remained for the duration of the War. During these years the pictures from the City Art Gallery were evacuated to Temple Newsam and there was a series of milestone exhibitions on Henry Moore, John Piper, Graham Sutherland and others which ensured that annual visitor numbers frequently exceeded 100,000. Hendy was succeeded by Ernest Musgrave (1946-1958) who pursued an energetic policy of acquisitions which transformed the collections, supported by a modest purchase grant, and by the Leeds Art Collections Fund (whose main remit at this time was to support modern art). The generally depressed state of the art market allowed some astonishing purchases to be made: Vasari's *St Jerome* (no 2) for £350 in 1954, Subleyras' *Horatio Walpole* (no 34) for £540 in 1957, Morland's ever-popular *Fair Nun* (no 40) for £375 in 1948, and Stubbs'

Phillis (no 36) for £450 in 1951. He also bought large canvases at Yorkshire country house sales: the French royal portraits from Cliffe Castle attributed to Francois de Troy (no 33) in 1950, the haunting Coccorante (no 28) from Hickleton Hall in 1947 and the Casteels (no 16) from Boynton Hall, also in 1950. Throughout this time there were also some important bequests: from the Armitage family of Farnley (nos 7 and 32), and above all Ernest Cook's ravishing Guardi (no 30) in 1955.

Robert Rowe (Director 1958-1983) continued the policy of acquiring Old Masters and was able to buy an important group of Italian Baroque pictures: Maratta's *St James* (no 18) from the Barberini collection in 1971, Gandolfi's *Christ and the Women taken in Adultery* (no 19) in 1961, and Matthias Stom's *Adoration of the Shepherds* (no 17) in 1967. He also continued to repatriate Temple Newsam 'heirlooms' when they became available: the Jolis (nos 25 and 26) in 1983. The return of historic pictures continued apace under Christopher Gilbert (Director 1983-1995), mainly in the area of portraits and continues as opportunities arise (no 24). Thus the loan and promised bequest of Sir Denis Mahon's *Rocky Landscape with a Hermit and a Lay Brother* (fig 4) by Pier Francesco Mola is especially appreciated. It now hangs in the place it occupied in the Picture Gallery in 1808, below Rubens' *Holy Family with St John the Baptist* (fig 3).

To visit the picture collection at Temple Newsam is a unique and authentic experience. Seen without the aid of much artificial light and dispersed among a large number of rooms with competing aesthetic attractions, the pictures may not have the same immediate impact as if they were hanging in a purpose-built art gallery. Nevertheless, to see them in this context is to view them through the eyes of a contemporary visitor: it is an experience which increases in enjoyment and value every time.

1 Adam and Eve

Flemish School, early 16TH century
(School of Jan van Scorel 1475-1562)

Oil on panel 23 × 17³/₄ in (58.5 × 45.1 cm)
Prov: Miss D Dawlish; Sotheby's 1.v.1946, lot 124; bought
from W Drown from the Harding Fund 1949 (£450) (3/49)

This extraordinarily interesting painting shows the multiplicity of different influences at work among northern European artists just at the moment when the High Renaissance was reaching its peak in Italy. The beautifully observed landscape is typically northern in the loving attention given to depicting the foreground plants and the peaceful woods. Its ethereal coolness recalls the work of the pioneer of landscape painting, Joachim Patinir (d c1524), and the graduated evening light determines the diminishing perspective in which the figures are set. But its composition appears to be based on a classically inspired drawing by Raphael engraved by Marcantonio Raimondi, while the figure style recalls Lucas Cranach (1472-1553).

The overwhelming atmosphere is one of imminent menace and threat. The first parents of the human race are shown in the Garden of Eden at the very moment they succumb to temptation and become guilty of Original Sin. Encouraged by Eve, Adam is about to eat the forbidden fruit: by crossing their legs both of them have become aware and ashamed of their nakedness. Although he is invisible the presence of the Serpent is implied in the strange shape of the trees. God's beautiful Creation is about to change forever: rabbits still play innocently in the undergrowth, swans glide elegantly on the river (both will become symbols of lust), while a resting hind (symbol of chastity) looks up in startled awareness of unholy events.

2 The Temptation of St Jerome

Giorgio Vasari (1511-1574)

Oil on panel 66½ x 47¼ in (168.3 x 119.4 cm)
Lit: G Vasari, *Vite…* (ed Milanesi), VII, p 669
Prov: Mrs Lungard; bought from C Marshall Spink 1954
(£350)(8/54)

St Jerome, or Eusebius Hieronymus Sophronius (320-420 AD), is one of the four traditional Doctors of the Church. His translation of the Bible into Latin, the Vulgate, was to become the official text of the Gospels for the Western Church.

The picture represents an episode in the saint's life when he retired for four years into the Syrian desert where he had 'only the scorpions and wild beasts for company'. He was a man of powerful intellect and fiery disposition who experienced violent sexual hallucinations. In one of his letters he described how he would beat his breast until the fever passed. A lion became his devoted companion after the saint removed a thorn from its paw.

In Vasari's autobiography the artist recorded painting two versions of this subject – one for Ottaviano de' Medici (now in Palazzo Pitti, Florence) and another in 1546 which was 'sent to France' (probably the picture here). He described it as *'lifesize… contemplating a crucifix and beating his breast, to drive away the lascivious thoughts that beset him in the wilderness, as he himself relates. To indicate this I did Venus fleeing with Cupid in her arms and leading Play, the quiver and arrows strewing the ground. Cupid's arrows lie broken and the doves of Venus pick up some with their beaks'.*

Giorgio Vasari, painter, architect and writer, was the great impresario of Renaissance art whose *Lives of the Most Eminent Architects, Painters and Sculptors* did much to encourage the high esteem in which Florentine art has subsequently been held. In particular he hero-worshipped Michelangelo.

3 Christ Carrying His Cross

Marco Palmezzano (c1460-1539)

Oil on panel 21 x 17 in (53.3 x 43.7 cm)
Signed and dated 1535 on paper on upright of cross
Given by W J Holt 1930 (3/30)

The painting is one of a number depicting this subject executed by Marco Palmezzano of Forli. The earliest is in Bonn and is signed and dated 1503; another is in the Vatican; a more elaborate variant with a landscape background and a soldier holding a rope attached to Christ's neck was on the art market in 1996.

The subject had a particular interest for the intense devotionalism of the late 15TH and early 16TH centuries; the resigned expression of the figure – whose cross symbolises the sins of the world – falls between the triumphalism of earlier representations of this subject and the naturalistic pathos of later artists' interpretations.

4 Portrait of a Young Man

Frans Pourbus the Younger (1569-1622)

Oil on panel 19¹/₂ x 14³/₄ in (49. x 37.5 cm)
Inscribed: (top left corner) *An: Dom 1591* and (top right corner) *Aetatis Suae 32/ Francisco Pourbus Fil' fr fecit*
Bought from G Neumann and given by a body of subscribers 1915 (258/15)

This arresting portrait of an unidentified young man aged 32 is one of the earliest known paintings by Frans Pourbus the Younger: his *Self Portrait* in the Uffizi, Florence also dates from 1591. He was from the third generation of a family of Flemish artists and was to become one of the most sought after royal portrait painters working for the Catholic courts of the early 17TH century, especially in Mantua, Spain and France. He was to have a considerable influence on Rubens.

The cool realism of this portrait, with its subtle use of directed light around the head and ruff, its carefully observed detail, and its psychological insight, is in sharp contrast to the hieratic style prevalent in England at this date. It was the genius of another Fleming, Anthony van Dyck, who was to transform this tradition and, by combining realism with formality, created some of the most brilliant images of pre-Civil War England.

5 Portrait of a Child with a Rattle

Possibly Henry Frederick Howard,
later third Earl of Arundel (1608-1652)
Attributed to Paul van Somer
(c1577-1621), dated 1611

Oil on panel 37³/₄ × 29 in (95.9 × 73.7 cm)
Given by the Rt Hon the Earl of Halifax 1948 (22.105/48)

This portrait probably first arrived at Temple
Newsam in the late 19TH century when it
was thought to represent Princess Elizabeth,
daughter of James I and Anne of Denmark,
and later Queen of Bohemia (the 'Winter
Queen'). Mrs Meynell Ingram, then the
owner of the house and the creator of the
Darnley Room, collected numerous items
associated with the early Stuarts in order to
promote this historic connection.

However, the evidence of the coat of arms
of the Howard family (Dukes of Norfolk) on
the back of the panel, together with the
incompatability of the Princess's age at the
time this picture was painted (1611), make it
much more likely that the young person is
Henry Frederick Howard, the future third
Earl of Arundel. A portrait of his father, the
celebrated collector Thomas Howard, second
Earl of Arundel, also hangs at Temple Newsam.

Henry later married Lady Elizabeth Stuart
whose grandfather Ludovic, second Duke of
Lennox was briefly the owner of Temple
Newsam before its purchase by Sir Arthur
Ingram in 1622. Henry was a staunch supporter
of the Royalist cause during the Civil War
and as a result much of his property was
impounded.

In this portrait he wears a magnificent
child's outfit (since he would not have been
breeched until about the age of six). It consists
of a bodice and skirt with appliquéd black
stripes, over which is an exceptionally fine lace
apron. He wears a chain with an Elizabethan
gold sovereign inscribed ELIZABETH DG ANG
FRA ET HIB REGINA. One hand holds a gilt
rattle while the other fondles some fruit in a
rare blue and white Chinese porcelain bowl.

Like Marcus Gheeraerts and Daniel Mytens,
both of whose work is also seen in the
collection, Paul van Somer was born in the Low
Countries but travelled extensively before
settling in London where he became the
favourite artist of Queen Anne of Denmark.

6 Eliezir and Rebecca at the Well

Flemish School, late 16TH century

Oil on panel 37 x 49 in (94 x 124.5 cm)
Lit: David Connell, 'Temple Newsam Paintings –
Discoveries and Reattributions', *Leeds Arts Calendar*,
no 110 (1992), pp 5-7
Prov: Given by the Rt Hon the Earl of Halifax 1948
(22.62/48)

The story is taken from Genesis, chapter 24. The patriarch Abraham, wishing to find a bride for his son Isaac, sent his servant Eliezir from Canaan where he lived into Mesopotamia. On reaching the city of Nahor in Chaldea he prayed that whoever was the first to give water to him and his camels would be an eligible woman. This proved to be Rebecca, a kinswoman of Abraham's who invited Eliezer to drink from her jar and drew water for his camels. Eliezer then gave her presents of gold and received hospitality from her parents' house. He brought her back to Canaan where Isaac, praying in the fields in the evening, saw them approach.

Although there are strong 'Italianising' details in this picture (the fountain, the costume of Rebecca and her maiden companions, and the elaborate ewer she holds), it is nevertheless faithful to the northern tradition in which the story is depicted as a continuous narrative meandering across the picture in an extended Z formation. The artist has not been identified but it was once attributed to Frans Floris (c1517-70). The same distinctive pyramidal camel packs with elephant tusks also appear in a drawing of this subject by Hans Bol (1534-93) suggesting that a number of artists may have used a common engraved source.

The painting is one of over 85 returned to Temple Newsam by Lord Halifax in 1948. It was first recorded here in the inventory of 1703 when it hung as a pendant to an *Abraham's Sacrifice* (now lost). It may have been in the collection much earlier as it is typical of the kind of paintings to be found in English houses since the late 16TH century.

7 Interior of Antwerp Cathedral

Peter Neefs the Younger (1620-1675)
or Elder (c1577-c1661)

Signed indistinctly and dated on first column on right 1653?
Oil on canvas 29 × 40 in (73.7 × 101.6 cm)
Given by the executors of Robert Armitage 1951 (8.2/51)

Church interiors were a favourite subject matter of Peter Neefs the Elder, a distinguished architectural painter from Antwerp, who was assisted and imitated by his son in his later years. In this example the signature on the first column on the right appears to be similar to those recorded for the son, although the father's authorship cannot be ruled out.

Views of large architectural interiors became popular in both northern and southern Netherlands in the 17TH century. Artists enjoyed the challenge of depicting complex perspectival scenes, real or imaginary, and often collaborating with other painters to fill them with elegant company.

8 Landscape with Sportsmen and Dogs

Paul Brill (1554-1626) and Jan Breughel
the Elder (c1568-1625)

Oil on copper 7 x 9 in (17.8 x 22.9 cm)
Signed on the reverse
Exhib: *The Cabinet Picture*, Richard Green Gallery,
London,1999 (ed C Wright, p 46)
Prov: Hamilton Palace sale, 20 July 1882, Fourth Portion
(lot 1058), bought by J A Rose for 21 guineas; bequeathed
by Charles Roberts through his wife Mrs B H Roberts
1965 (24.25/65)

This beautifully wrought small painting is
a classic example of a Cabinet Picture, so
called for their original purpose of decorating a 'cabinet' or small intimate room in
the house of a connoisseur. Cabinet Pictures
were characterised by their small scale and
exquisite quality, and were intended to thrill
the eye of the spectator rather than impart
any other message. This example (and its
pendant an *Italian Landscape* by Bartholomeus
Breenbergh also at Temple Newsam 24.26/65)
have a most distinguished provenance: they
may well have formed part of the collection of William Beckford, one of the most
discerning of all English connoisseurs. His
daughter married the tenth Duke of Hamilton
whose successor sold them in 1882 at one of
the most famous art sales of the 19TH century
at Hamilton Palace, near Glasgow.

At Temple Newsam similar Dutch and
Italian cabinet pictures were acquired by suc-
cessive Viscounts Irwin in the 18TH century.
Instead of being hung in a small intimate
room they were, for the most part, displayed
in the Picture Gallery at eye level, below the
full length portraits and other large scale
subject paintings.

Paul Brill, from Antwerp, lived almost all
his life in Rome where this was painted in the
1590s. He was most celebrated for jewel-like
landscapes painted on copper, depicting woods,
waterfalls and hunting figures, although he
later worked on a larger scale. His style
was very influential in the development of
landscape painting which was evolving among
the international group of artists living in
Rome at this time. It has been suggested that
the figures in this painting may be by Jan
('Velvet') Breughel the Elder with whom Brill
sometimes collaborated.

9 Floral Studies:
Carnations in a Vase

Balthasar van der Ast (c1593-1657)

Signed bottom left
Oil on panel 13 × 10¾ in (33.5 × 27 cm)
Allocated to Leeds Art Galleries by HM Treasury
in lieu of taxes 1987 (48.1/87)

10 Floral Studies with Beaker,
Grasshopper and Seashells

Balthasar van der Ast (c1593-1657)

Oil on panel 14 × 10½ in (37 × 26.1 cm)
Allocated to Leeds Art Galleries by HM Treasury
in lieu of taxes 1987 (48.2/87)

These two paintings, not necessarily conceived
as pendants, represent the finest achievement
of Dutch flower painting of the early 17TH
century. The beautifully observed detail of
the different floral species shows the obses-
sion with botanical and scientific enquiry so
characteristic of the age, while the flowers
themselves, with their accompanying shells
and grasshopper, speak of the transience
of life.

11 Still Life with Dead Game

Willem van Aelst (1627-c1683)

Oil on canvas 38 x 30 in (96.5 x 76.2 cm)
Signed and dated 1673 bottom left
Exhib: *Dutch Seventeenth Century Paintings from Yorkshire Public Collections*, Leeds City Art Gallery 1983 (9)
Given by Mrs E Fawcett 1931 (16/31)

In contrast to the lightness and clarity of Dutch still life painting in the earlier period artists of the later 17TH century preferred a darker tonality, often treating their more sombre subject matter with exaggerated Baroque 'movement'. Dutch artists in particular refined their technique towards a more highly polished effect, sometimes with spectaculary illusionistic results.

Willem van Aelst, from Delft, specialised in still life and flower painting. He worked extensively for the Medici of Florence for whom he produced a series of still life pictures of hunting trophies and equipment.

12 Portrait of a Man with Grey Hair
Attributed to Adriaen Hanneman
(1601-1671)

Oil on canvas 30 × 25 in (76.2 × 63.5 cm)
Bought from Mr A Asscher from the Corporation Fund
1953 (£250) (4/53)

This distinguished portrait of an unidentified man is close in style to the work of Adriaen Hanneman, the Dutch artist who spent several years of his youth in London where he may have worked as an assistant to Anthony van Dyck. On returning to Holland he continued to work in the van Dyck manner, especially among the exiled English royalists. Here the furtive glance in the sitter's eyes, the turn of his head, his cascading grey hair and crumpled collar picked out with highlights convey an impression of tension and nervousness.

13 Two Seated Figures with a Dog
Attributed to Michael Sweerts
(1618-1664)

Oil on board 18½ x 15 in (47.2 x 37.5 cm)
Bequeathed by M Preston 1976 (36.1/76)

Michael Sweerts was a Fleming who, like many artists of the 17TH century from the Low Countries, travelled and worked in Rome. Here he was greatly influenced by the so-called *bamboccianti* who specialised in scenes of peasants and low life, often with a narrative or anecdotal content. Sweerts' scenes are distinctive for the almost sculptural monumentality of the figures, derived from his studies of classical sculpture.

14 Storm off Egmond aan Zee

Jacob van Ruisdael (1628-1682)

Oil on canvas 41 x 57 in (106.2 x 147.3 cm)
Exhib and Lit: Alexander Robertson and Christopher
Wright, *Dutch Seventeenth Century Paintings from Yorkshire
Public Collections*, Leeds City Art Gallery 1982-83 (37)
Bought from Assher and Walker from the Hoffman
Wood Bequest 1935 (£900) (2/35)

Ruisdael is often considered the greatest of all Dutch landscape painters even though he lacks the charm or atmosphere of Hobbema or van Goyen. His subjects seem very directly observed, stark and devoid of any picturesque detail. He rarely painted a sunny day or included charming anecdotes in his compositions.

This scene evokes a dramatic storm with the threatening grey sky counterbalancing the dark turbulence of the sea. The spectator gradually becomes aware of the majestic rawness of nature.

15 Still Life with Fruit
Maximilian Pfeiler (fl 1683-1706)

Oil on canvas 25 × 31 in (63.5 × 78.5 cm)
Signed and dated 1706 on stone slab on left
Given by the Earl of Halifax 1948 (22.100/48)

This is one of a pair of *Still Life* paintings by Maximilian Pfeiler almost certainly acquired by Henry, fourth Viscount Irwin of Temple Newsam while on his Grand Tour 1704-7. They are mentioned in all the subsequent inventories of the pictures in the house.

Pfeiler was a German artist who worked in Rome, specialising in this genre. One of the paintings is dated 1706, suggesting that Lord Irwin bought them while visiting the city that year. From all accounts the symbolism of the luscious over-ripeness of the fruit would not have been lost on this young English nobleman.

16 Fantastic Still Life in a Classical Landscape
Peter Casteels (1684-1749)

Oil on canvas 32½ x 32½ in (82.5 x 82.5 cm)
Signed and dated 1708 bottom left
Exhib: *The Irresistible Object: Still Life 1600-1985*,
Leeds City Art Gallery 1985 (14); *Manners and Morals:
Hogarth and British Painting 1700-1760*, Tate Gallery
1988 (47)
Prov: Painted for Sir William Strickland of Boynton Hall,
Yorkshire; bought at the Boynton Hall sale, Henry
Spencer and Sons 22.xi.50 (lot 386) (£400) (42.6/50)

Despite its popularity in Holland and else-where in the 17TH and early 18TH centuries still life painting never achieved such high esteem among the English, with their love of portraits and sporting art. Nevertheless, with the development of formal Baroque interiors such paintings were often commissioned as decorative overdoors or overmantels, usually executed by foreigners.

The perfectly square format of this picture betrays its original function as an overmantel. It is a late example of the genre (c1730),

suggesting certain Rococo tendencies in the casual yet unusually busy combination of flowers, dead game, architecture and landscape. It was probably intended to hang at Sir William Strickland's house at Boynton Hall, near Bridlington, Yorkshire, c1730 when the owner was undertaking alterations under the supervision of William Kent who designed its frame. Shortly afterwards the frame design was reproduced in *Designs of Inigo Jones and Others* (1735) also showing its pediment (now lost).

17 The Adoration of the Shepherds
Matthias Stom (c1600-1656)

Oil on canvas 49 x 69 in (124.5 x 175.5 cm)
Lit: Terry F Friedman, 'Allegory in Stomer's *The Adoration of the Shepherds*', *Leeds Arts Calendar*, no 81 (1977), pp 5-9
Exhib: *Matthias Stom, Isaac Blessing Jacob*, Barber Institute, University of Birmingham 1999
Prov: Bought from P and D Colnaghi with the aid of a government grant (9/67)

'And they came with haste, and found Mary, and Joseph, and the babe lying in a manger'

The scene, one of the most familiar yet most potent in the repertory of Christian imagery, is interpreted here in a most unusual way and with a number of hidden symbols. To the right, in the half light, is Joseph whose face is thrown into a second shadow by a trick of the light; this second profile has the features of the future apostle St Peter who is thus staring at the cockerel being held by one of the shepherds – a reference to his later Denial of Christ. Less obvious is the cross formed on Mary's red mantle by the shadow of the swaddling clothes bisected at right angles by her left arm.

The artist, Matthias Stom (or Stomer), was born in the Low Countries but left for Italy in c1603. Here he came under the powerful influence of Michelangelo Merisi da Caravaggio (1573-1610) which was then sweeping Europe. Caravaggio's art centred on *'types chosen from the common people, his magic realism and light revealing a passionate belief that it was the simple in spirit, the humble and poor who held the mysteries of faith fast within their souls'*. In this picture the peasant-like features of the figures are dramatically highlighted by the glowing light which emanates from the baby Jesus, which is indeed the only source of light in the entire picture.

This picture was probably painted in Naples during the years in which Stom worked in the city, between 1633 and 1639. There are at least eleven versions of this subject, each with small variations.

F.108.

18 St James the Greater
Carlo Maratta (1625-1713)

Oil on canvas 87¹/₂ × 59 in (222 × 149 cm)
Inscribed with Palazzo Barberini inventory no F.108
(for 1631, 1692-1704)
Lit: Alexander Robertson, 'St James the Greater: a
Painting by Carlo Maratta', *Leeds Arts Calendar* no 75
(1974) pp 19-22
Bought from Colnaghi's from the Corporation Fund with
the aid of a government grant 1971 (£8,500) (24/71)

This is one from a series of paintings of the twelve apostles ordered in 1661 by Cardinal Antonio Barberini for the family palace in Rome. His original choice of artist was Andrea Sacchi who finished a *St Peter* before he died, whereupon the commission was handed over to his follower Carlo Maratta.

Cardinal Barberini and his brother Pope Urban VIII (reigned 1623-1644) were brilliant patrons of the arts, responsible for some of the most memorable buildings, fountains and monuments of Baroque Rome. At Palazzo Barberini, among other achievements, they commissioned two leading painters to decorate the principal rooms: Pietro da Cortona and Andrea Sacchi. The former painted an extravagant Baroque *Allegory of Divine Providence* for the salone, with swirling figures and on an epic scale; the latter chose a more Classical approach with fewer figures shown in dignified poses. This polarisation of attitudes, Baroque versus Classical, was a source of much debate among critics at the time.

Maratta's style, as can be seen here, was closer to Sacchi's. The whole series, when hung together, must have been very striking: the grandeur of the single figures, their simple but commanding poses, the cloaks brilliant in colour and harmony are all expertly handled. The result is very much in accord with the theory that a whole work of art should consist of the selection of beautiful parts rather than any preconceived notion of beauty.

The apostle is dressed as a pilgrim, holding a staff and enjoining his unseen companions towards their sacred destination. It refers to his own cult at Compostella where his relics have been venerated for centuries.

19 Christ and the Woman taken in Adultery

Gaetano Gandolfi (1734-1802)

Oil on canvas 37 x 44 in (94 x 111.8 cm)
Exhib: *Mostra del 700 Bolognese*, Palazzo Communale, Bologna 1935 (Sala 9, no 9); *Light of the World: Christ's Story Told Through Art*, City Art Centre, Edinburgh 1999 (7)
Lit: Donatella Biagi Maino, *Gaetano Gandolfi* (1995)
Bought from Sotheby's 14 June 1961 (lot 78) (£1,870) with the aid of a government grant (3/61)

The subject is taken from St John's Gospel when an adulteress is brought before Christ by the Scribes and Pharisees who were hoping to trap Him into either violating the Law of Moses by refusing to condemn her, or betraying His own doctrine of forgiveness. The artist has chosen the moment when Christ tells the accusers that they have the right to stone her only if they themselves are without sin.

Gaetano Gandolfi was the pupil of his elder brother Ubaldo and is often considered the last major figure of the great period of Bolognese painting. He studied in Venice where he admired the work of Veronese and of Gian Battista and Gian Domenico Tiepolo. This work probably dates from the same period as his masterpiece *The Marriage of Cana* (signed and dated 1775) originally painted for the Convent of San Salvatore, Bologna and now in the Pinacoteca there. The same figure of Christ appears in this picture and the same figure of the adulteress appears in a *Judgement of Solomon*. The young man in the left background may be a self portrait.

20 The Baptism of Christ

Francesco Trevisani (1656-1746)

Oil on canvas 97 1/2 x 75 in (247.6 x 190.5 cm)
Signed and dated 1723 (bottom left)
Given by G W Brown 1915 (286/15)

'And it came to pass in those days that Jesus came from Nazareth of Galilee and was baptised by John in the river Jordan. And straightaway coming up out of the water He saw the heavens opened and the Spirit like a dove descending upon Him. And there came a voice from heaven saying "Thou art my beloved Son in whom I am well pleased".'

This painting was almost certainly commissioned as an altarpiece for a side chapel or a provincial church under the protection of Cardinal Pietro Ottoboni (1667-1740) whose coat of arms appear in the lower left-hand corner. Ottoboni, nephew of Pope Alexander VIII, was a discerning intellectual and patron of artists and craftsmen, including Trevisani, living in great splendour at Palazzo della Cancelleria in Rome. A striking portrait of him also by Trevisani is at the Bowes Museum. English clients included members of the exiled Jacobite court and Grand Tourists such as Sir Edward Gascoigne whose portrait may be seen at Lotherton Hall (Leeds Museums and Galleries).

Trevisani inherited the mantle of Maratta (see no 18) as one of the leading artists in Rome after the latter's death in 1713. In this fine example of his late style he came to unite the drama and *chiaroscuro* of the earlier Baroque masters with the clarity of organisation and fresh colouring of the Classicists.

21 Hector and Andromache
Giovanni Antonio Pellegrini (1675-1741)

Oil on canvas 92 × 88 in (233 × 223.5 cm)
Lit: Edward Croft-Murray, *Decorative Painting in England
1537-1837* (1970), II pp 253-256; George Knox,
Antonio Pellegrini 1675-1741 (1995)
Prov: The Dukes of Manchester at Kimbolton Castle;
bought from Leggatt Brothers 1959 (£2,000) with a
contribution from the National Art Collections Fund (9/59)

The subject is a popular one taken from Homer's *Iliad*: Hector, the commander of the Trojan forces says farewell to his wife Andromache and their son Astyanax on the eve of battle. The child is frightened by the sight of the plumed helmet and shrinks back into his father's arms.

The painting was almost certainly commissioned by the first Duke of Manchester who brought Pellegrini to England from his native Venice in 1708. The artist was responsible for decorating the Duke's seat at Kimbolton Castle in a spirited late Baroque style: this painting was recorded there in 1770 hanging over the chimney piece in the Saloon.

Pellegrini was one of a small group of foreign artists working in England in the early years of the 18TH century, encouraged by the possibilty of decorating the newly completed dome of St Paul's Cathedral. In the event none of them was chosen, but their legacy remains in a number of large scale country house schemes.

22 The Choice of Hercules
Paolo de Matteis (1662-1728)

Oil on canvas 25 × 30 in (64.1 × 76.8 cm)
Signed and dated 1712 on the stone bottom centre
Lit: Sheila O'Connell, 'Lord Shaftesbury in Naples
1711-1713', *Walpole Society Journal*, Vol 54 for 1988
(1991), pp 149-219
Prov: Sir John Cropley and by descent to the Wood
family; given by the Earl of Halifax 1948 (22.15/48)

The subject is taken from classical mythology when the great hero Hercules, before he embarked on his twelve labours *'retired to a solitary place in order to deliberate on the choice he was to make of the different ways of life [where he] was accosted… by the two Goddesses, Virtue and Pleasure'*. They offered him either a life of dissipation, or of duty. Here Hercules is seen looking towards Virtue (left) while his body still leans towards Pleasure (right).

The picture is a reduced size contemporary replica of the original painted in Naples for the Earl of Shaftesbury in 1712 (now in the Ashmolean Museum, Oxford). It became famous through an engraving published in the latter's highly influential book *Characteristicks of Men, Manners, Opinions, Times* which contained a treatise on history painting and the heroic style entitled *A Notion of the Historical Draught or Tablature of the Judgment of Hercules*. In this he describes the moral and philosophical implications of 'the grand manner' in painting and the importance of the unities of time, action and place by reference to this picture. The high-mindedness of its subject was ideal for demonstrating Shaftesbury's theories.

A series of letters describes how Shaftesbury dictated precisely to the artist Paolo de Matteis how the composition should be arrived at, as well as the gestures of the figures and the colours. A number of preliminary sketches were made before the painting was finished and the artist received his fee of 360 ducats.

The Temple Newsam picture was finished by 29 June 1712, three months after the original, and the artist received a further 120 ducats (£24). It was intended to be a gift to Shaftesbury's patron Lord Somers but in the event it was bought by Shaftesbury's friend Sir John Cropley. Shaftesbury wrote to him that *'there will be no need of a carved, gilded or otherwise expensive frame: it must be plain and of dark coloured wood, not shining'*. The present gilt frame dates from the late 18TH century: the frame on the original painting at Oxford is a celebrated example of virtuoso carving in an advanced Rococo style.

23 Seascape with Shipwreck

Antonio Marini (1668-1725)

Oil on canvas 67 × 102 in (170 × 259 cm)
Lit: Christopher Gilbert, 'A Nobleman and the Grand
Tour: Lord Irwin and Marco Ricci', *Apollo*, vol lxxxiii, no 51
(May 1966), pp358-363; Maria Silvia Proni, *Antonio Maria Marini: l'opera completa* (1992)
Given by the Rt Hon the Earl of Halifax 1948 (22.84/48)

This dramatic painting is one of a group originally numbering about 40 which arrived at Temple Newsam in 1709 having been commissioned by Edward fourth Viscount Irwin while on his Grand Tour of Europe 1704-7. The majority depict stormy landscapes, seascapes and battle scenes. The artist had been forgotten since the middle of the 18TH century and has only recently been identified as the highly esteemed Paduan, Antonio Marini. This is based on a recently discovered signature on a closely related landscape painting in the Accademia Carrara, Bergamo. Marini also included his own *Self Portrait* in this consignment (see no 24).

After succeeding his father at the age of 15 and completing his education at Eton and Cambridge, Edward Lord Irwin (1686-1714) departed for the Continent together with his brother Richard, his tutor John Haccius and a friend Thomas Worsley. Travelling through Holland and Germany they passed the winter of 1706-7 in Venice spending money lavishly on works of art. He wrote home to his mother requesting more funds and probably referring to these pictures:

'I beg your Ladyship too to consider what I have bought since I have been abroad for ye ornament of my house, as pictures, books and ye like I have laid out three hundred pounds... so I desire your Ladyship will hasten me a bill of ye said three hundred pounds so that I may not be obliged to stay in this place beyond ye time I propose myself... After this I am persuaded you won't think I have spent my money foolishly. I should have continued buying, but that I find my circumstances won't allow it which I confess vexes me; for I have a good opportunity of furnishing my great rambling house with excellent paintings for two or three hundred pounds more if I had it...'

His pleas must have been heard since over £800 was laid out to cover his expenses while he was in the city. Over 40 paintings were despatched to England – their final journey being by sea from Rotterdam to Hull where customs duties of £11-19-11d were paid.

All the pictures are in pairs of different sizes, evidently intended to hang as pendants. Thus from the outset the whole group were intended to create a comprehensive display comparable to the decorative ensembles devised for fashionable Italian interiors. They were probably given their uniform Palladian frames when the remodelled Gallery was completed in 1745 or 1746. Several individual pictures were removed or sold in 1922.

The paintings represent an interesting phase in the development of Italian landscape painting, bridging the period between Salvator Rosa's wild and romantic scenes and Francesco Guardi's ethereal views. Lord Irwin's taste for this kind of painting was most unusual. At this time most English grand tourists were buying highly finished classical landscapes in the style of Claude and Poussin, or history paintings in the grand manner. It was only later in the 18TH century that the 'sublime' or tempestuous quality of these paintings was to become an important influence on the development of landscape gardening in Britian.

24 Self Portrait

Antonio Marini (1668-1725)

Oil on canvas 28 × 21 in (71 × 53.5 cm)
Lit: David Connell, 'Temple Newsam Paintings – Discoveries and Reattributions', *Leeds Arts Calendar*, no 110 (1992), p 11; Maria Silvia Proni, *Antonio Maria Marini, l'opera completa* (1992), p 50
Bought 1998 with the aid of grants from the National Art Collections Fund and the MGC/V&A Purchase Grant Fund (£23,491 after tax remission)(1998.0022)

This remarkable *Self Portrait* almost certainly arrived at Temple Newsam in 1709 in the same consignment of 'about 40' paintings of landscapes, seascapes and battle scenes ordered by Henry, fourth Viscount Irwin in Venice two years earlier (see no 23).

Their authorship was soon forgotten but they are now recognised as the work of the Paduan artist Antonio Marini. This *Self Portrait* must have been included in the series since 'An Italian artist's head' is recorded in every inventory of the house until 1922. No wonder, for Lord Irwin's commission was probably the most important in Marini's career.

Marini has given a spirited and dramatic rendering of his own image in which his head and hands stand out in strong light against a darkened background. His sleeve, cuff and cravat display his characteristic style of vigorous and swiftly applied brushstrokes. The composition of oblique converging lines is typical of his work and give an extraordinary sense of immediacy. The gesture of the artist's right hand seems to beckon the spectator towards Lord Irwin's paintings as though they were still hanging just out of sight on the walls of the studio.

25 View on the Tiber

Antonio Joli (c1700-1770)

Oil on canvas 42 x 48 1/2 in (106.7 x 123.2 cm)
Signed on a box on the riverbank
Accepted by H M Treasury in lieu of taxes and allocated
to remain in situ at Temple Newsam 1983 (30.1/83)

These two paintings were acquired by Henry, seventh Viscount Irwin of Temple Newsam in c1745 to hang as overmantels in his newly completed Saloon or Picture Gallery. They are visually integral to each fireplace which were made after a design of William Kent by the master sculptor Robert Doe of London.

Antonio Joli, from Modena, trained in Rome under the master of ruin pictures G P Panini (see no 27) and also worked as a scene painter. In Venice he came into contact with the topographical art of Canaletto. Like the latter, he travelled extensively in Europe and was in London between 1744 and 1748 where presumably he met Lord Irwin. Later he settled in Naples where his views and scenes of ceremonies were highly sought after, especially among the English Grand Tourists.

St Peter's cannot be seen from this position on the river Tiber. Joli has 're-arranged' it for a more artistic effect.

26 Architectural Fantasy

(also known as *The Pool of Bethseda*)

Antonio Joli (c1700-1770)

See opposite for details
Unsigned (30.2/83)

In contrast to the *View on the Tiber,* the *Architectural Fantasy,* showing figures bathing among the ruins of Roman baths, is entirely imaginary. In the 1808 inventory it was described as *'The Pool of Bethseda'* (sic) where Christ performed the miracle of the Healing of the Paralytic. In St John's Gospel Bethesda was described as 'a place with five colonnades' where the sick came to bathe: it was believed that from time to time the Archangel Raphael came and disturbed the waters and the first person to enter thereafter would be cured. The paralytic had never succeeded in being first: so Christ ordered him to take up his bed and walk and immediately he recovered.

27 Roman Ruins with the Blind Belisarius

Gian Paolo Panini (1691-1765)

Oil on canvas 56 × 52 in (142.3 × 132.1 cm)
Signed and dated 1730 on foreground stone
Given by J G Uppleby 1858 (249/1858)

Ruin pictures or *capricci* of Rome, incorporating views of well-known or imaginary monuments of Antiquity, were bought avidly by Grand Tourists in the 18TH century.

G P Panini had a particularly successful studio specialising in such scenes, often contriving to re-arrange the ruins. Here, the Coloseum is seen behind the Arch of Titus and an invented colonnade, and in the foreground is the Temple of Fortuna Virilis and a version of the famous Borghese Vase.

In contrast to Coccorante (no 28) whose ruin pictures evoke a sinister twilight world, Panini sought to combine intimations of transience in a more decorative mode. His figures often contribute to this theme: in the foreground here the blind and discredited general Belisarius, whose campaigns had once regained huge tracts of territory for the Empire, is discovered begging among the ruins by a group of soldiers.

Somewhat later in the 18TH century, after the publication of Edmund Gibbon's *Decline and Fall of the Roman Empire* and the loss of the American Colonies, the English (who considered themselves to be the true heirs to the Roman Empire) were to find much to meditate upon when confronted with the ruins of *'Roma Immortalis'*.

OPPOSITE

28 Imaginary Ruins

Leonardo Coccorante (1680-1750)
(figures possibly by Giuseppe Tomajuoli,
active 1730-49)

Oil on canvas 80 × 71 in (203.2 × 180.3 cm)
Signed in monogram LC bottom left
Prov: Lord Grimthorpe; Christie's 12 May 1906;
Viscount Halifax; sold Hickleton Hall sale Hollis and Webb
18 March 1947, lot 461; bought from the Corporation
Fund (30 guineas) (13.1/47)

Works by the Neapolitan ruin painter Leonardo Coccorante are much rarer than the more decorative views by his better known contemporary Gian Paolo Panini (no 27). The genre of Roman ruin pictures dates back to the 15TH century but acquired new meaning for Grand Tourists of the 18TH century who bought them as souvenirs of their Italian travels. They were either considered to be decorative wall coverings or, more profoundly, to inspire reflection on the transience of empires.

Coccorante is said to have begun his career as a jailer's assistant and was taught his craft by a Sicilian painter of architectual subjects from Palermo who had been imprisoned for burglary, Angelo Maria Costa.

Coccorante's interpretation is considerably more poetic and dramatic than his contemporaries Panini and Joli (nos 27, 25 and 26), especially in his use of deep shadows and *chiaroscuro*. His figures are going about their everyday business in an eerie, sinister atmosphere: the soaring ruins and stairs are used almost as a theatrical backdrop while the dilapidated fountain doubles as a funerary monument with a figure of a river god and an obelisk.

29 Allegory of Autumn (Ceres)
Andrea Casali (1705-1784)

Oil on canvas 36 x 28 in (91.5 x 71.1 cm)
Bequeathed by Mrs A E Bateson 1950 (18.7/50)

The allegory shows Ceres, the Greek goddess of agriculture, together with a young follower of Bacchus, god of wine, representing the fruits of the earth at harvest-time or autumn.

The picture is one of a set of four depicting the Seasons which were originally painted as overdoors for Fonthill Splendens, Wiltshire, the country house of a former Lord Mayor of London, Alderman Beckford which was re-built after a fire c1755. It was demolished c1807 when his son, the infamous connoisseur William Beckford, built the more famous Fonthill Abbey nearby. It would seem that the four paintings were probably sold and split up a few years later. *Spring* and *Summer* are now at the Holburne of Menstrie Museum, Bath, while *Winter* remains untraced.

Andrea Casali was one of a number of Italian artists who came to England in search of a market for their skills in the mid-18TH century and who are well represented at Temple Newsam: Giovanni Antonio Pellegrini (no 21), Antonio Joli (nos 25 and 26) and Antonio Canaletto. He was a pupil of Francesco Trevisani (see no 20) and arrived in England c1741. Alderman Beckford was one of his major clients and other works formerly at Fonthill can be seen at Burton Constable, Yorkshire and Dyrham Park, Gloucestershire.

30 S Giorgio Maggiore
Francesco Guardi (1712-1793)

Oil on canvas 18³/₄ × 34¹/₂ in (47.6 × 87.6 cm)
Prov: painted for John Ingram, Palazzo Mignanelli, Rome;
his daughter Margaret Godfrey; A H Godfrey;
sold Christie's 15 March 1929 (lot 89); Goodden and Fox;
Ernest Cook (1933); bequeathed to the National Art
Collections Fund and presented to Leeds 1955 (as *On the
Lagoon, Venice*) (16.1/55)

Guardi's views of Venice evolved from the topographical tradition popularised by his probable master Antonio Canaletto. Guardi's concern was to capture the poetry of the city and its lagoon by using flickering nervous brushstrokes and by exaggerating the atmospheric effects of its unique light.

On the left of the view is the famous church and monastery of S Giorgio Maggiore (built by Andrea Palladio from 1566), with its campanile (which collapsed in 1774). To the right is the island of the Giudecca with the campanile of S Giovanni Battista and the dome of the church of the Zitelle (S Maria della Presentazione).

There are at least seven different versions of this view painted by Guardi probably in the early 1770s, including examples in the Wallace Collection, Penrhyn Castle, Toledo (Ohio) and the Accademia (Venice). In addition he made at least three drawings and an etching of this scene.

This picture was formerly owned by Ernest Cook, the descendant of the original travel agent Thomas Cook, who beqeathed his works of art to the National Art Collections Fund in 1955 for distribution to museums throughout Britain.

31 Allegory of Europe

Studio of Francesco Solimena
(1657-1747)

Oil on canvas 37 × 28³/₄ in (94 × 73 cm)
Lit: Kim Sloan, 'Sir William Hamilton's Insuperable Taste
for Painting', *Journal of the History of Collections* 9 no 2
(1997) pp 205-227
Prov: Sir William Hamilton; sold Christie's 17 April 1801
(lot 50 'two oval sketches'); bought by Sir Francis Wood;
by descent to the Earl of Halifax who gave them 1948
(22.25/48)

This sketch is a pendant to a similar *Allegory
of Africa*, also at Temple Newsam, and was
probably originally part of a group of four,
with *Asia* and *America*. They are derived from
fresco paintings representing the *Four Parts
of the World*, painted by Solimena for the
Gabinetto of the royal palace in Naples. Other
sets have survived, including one at Palazzo
Doria in Rome.

Europe is depicted as an imperious but
benign figure of universal authority bringing
peace to the world: with her right hand
she helps support a Renaissance tempietto,
symbolising the universal Church, while behind
her to her left the banners of ancient Rome
(inscribed SPQR) lend her the legitimacy of
antiquity. With her left hand she points to the
power and authority vested in the triple tiara
and the crown of the Holy Roman Empire.
Beneath her feet are the vanquished arms
of warfare while the dove of peace appears
above. The same female model appears in other
(less elevating) subjects by Solimena.

Early in their history the paintings came
into the possession of Sir William Hamilton,
the British envoy in Naples in the late 18TH
century. As well as being the husband of the
infamous Emma, mistress of Lord Nelson, he
was a celebrated collector of paintings and
ancient vases.

32 The Raising of Lazarus

Christian Wilhelm Ernst Dietrich

(1712-1774)

Oil on canvas 43 × 35 in (109.2 × 88.9 cm)
Signed on stone bottom left
Lit: (for Epinal version) *La Revue du Louvre*, 1983 nos 3, 5/6
Prov: Armitage family of Farnley Hall, Farnley Moor,
Leeds; given by the executors of R Armitage 1951
(8.1/51)

This unusual pastiche of an early Rembrandt
by the Dresden artist C W E Dietrich testifies
to the former's enduring popularity in the
18TH century. The *Gemaldegalerie* at Dresden,
of which Dietrich became Inspector, was
founded as a publicly accessible art gallery
by Augustus the Strong in the early 18TH
century and was famous for its large number
of paintings by Rembrandt. Interestingly there
is a fine copy of Rembrandt's *Portrait of Saskia*
by another 18TH century Dresden copyist,
J A J Franke, at Temple Newsam.

During the 18TH century the owners
of Temple Newsam acquired at least two
'Rembrandts': a fine *Self Portrait* (Private
Collection, on loan to William de Young
Memorial Museum, San Francisco), and a
version of the Louvre, *Supper at Emmaus* (still
at Temple Newsam).

33 The duchesse de la Ferté with the duc d'Anjou (later Louis XV) and the duc de Bretagne
Attributed to François de Troy
(1645-1730)

Oil on canvas 66 x 60¼ in (167.7 x 153 cm)
Lit: William Wells, 'A Royal Portrait from the hotel de la
Ferté', *Leeds Arts Calendar*, no 18 (1952), pp 23-32
Prov: Louis Jean Gaignat; The Earl of Lonsdale (Christie's
18 July 1887, lot 856); Mr Morgan; Butterfield family;
Countess Manvers; bought at the Cliffe Castle sale,
Hollis and Webb, 5-8 June 1950 (lot 353) (£250) (23/50)

The figures in this painting are almost certainly the duchesse de la Ferté with, on her lap, the infant duc d'Anjou (later Louis xv), and his elder brother, the duc de Bretagne who died in 1712. Both boys were great-grandchildren of Louis xiv by their father the duc de Bourgogne.

The picture was first recorded in the sale catalogue of the hotel de la Ferté in 1768 when it was one of a series of six forming part of the decoration of a room. All the companion pictures (except one) were portraits of the hereditary governesses to the French royal family, which post had descended by inheritance through the female line from the marquise de Lansac, governess to Louis xiv. Two of these companion portraits have survived: one, of madame de Lansac at Versailles, and another of madame de Ventadour and the duc de Bretagne in a private collection.

In contrast to the companion portraits which depict the royal governesses, this picture almost certainly represents a royal godmother — the duchesse de la Ferté, a sister of the then royal governess madame de Ventadour — who performed this duty in 1712 when the two princes contracted measles and had to be baptised at short notice. The elder boy, the duc de Bretagne, died some days later, leaving the infant duc d'Anjou as the sole heir of his great-grandfather Louis xiv. This picture was therefore probably commisssioned by the duchess to commemorate her relationship with these two members of the royal family and to join the others in the set illustrating her family's long association with the crown. The garland of flowers held above the elder boy may be an allusion to his premature death.

34 Portrait of Horatio Walpole

Second Baron Walpole of Wolterton;
first Earl of Orford of the second creation
Pierre Subleyras (1699-1749)

Oil on canvas 38¹/₂ x 29¹/₄ in (96.5 x 73.7 cm)
Signed on paper to the left
Lit: James Lomax, 'Prince Pigwiggin in Italy',
Leeds Arts Calendar no 83 (1978), pp 9-19
Exhib: *Subleyras* 1699-1749, Musee du Luxembourg,
Paris and Villa Medici, Rome 1987
Prov: Montague L Meyer (Avon Castle 1946); bought
(Corporation Fund) from Arthur Tooth and Sons 1957
(£540) (15/57)

Horatio Walpole came from the well-known
Norfolk family who rose to prominence
in the early 18TH century when his uncle,
Sir Robert Walpole, became Prime Minister.
His father was a diplomat and ambassador to
France and was created first Baron Walpole
of Wolterton; his cousin, Horace Walpole of
Strawberry Hill – with whom he was *not* on
friendly terms – was the famous wit and man
of letters.

Young Horatio (1723-1809) was sent on
the Grand Tour together with his tutor
the Rev George Turnbull in 1745. The latter
had been instructed to report back any
suspicious movements of the Jacobites who
they encountered on their travels. They
journeyed via Turin and Florence, reaching
Rome by April 1746 where this portrait
must have been painted.

The choice of Subleyras was an inspired
one, but not shared by many English grand
tourists. Subleyras was born near Avignon
and moved to Rome as an art student in
1727 where he remained for the rest of his
life. His work generally consists of large scale
religious and history pictures, although he also
painted fine portraits of Pope Benedict XIV,
members of the papal court and the Roman
nobility. This painting should be compared
with others executed by fashionable portrait
painters in Rome in the 18TH century: Sir
Edward Gascoigne by Francesco Trevisani and
Sir Thomas Gascoigne by Pompeo Batoni,
both at Lotherton Hall (also owned by Leeds
Museums and Galleries).

35 Portrait of Lady Jenkinson
Philip Mercier (1689-1760)

Oil on canvas 99¹/₂ × 59¹/₂ in (252.7 × 151.1 cm)
Inscribed, signed and dated 1742 bottom left
Given by the Earl of Halifax 1948 (22.112/48)

Henrietta Jenkinson (1695-1760) was the eldest daughter of Charles Scarburgh of Windsor and grand-daughter of the royal physician Sir Charles Scarburgh. She was Lady-in-Waiting to Queen Anne 1709-12 and married Sir Robert Jenkinson Bt of Walcot, Oxfordshire in 1717. Her two sisters, Anne and Elizabeth, were married to the two Ingram brothers: Henry, seventh Viscount Irwin of Temple Newsam and Colonel the Hon Charles Ingram. After the death of Lady Jenkinson's husband she came to live at Temple Newsam where no doubt she and her sisters constituted a considerable power in determining the affairs of the household. They were probably largely responsible for the floral needlework which still adorns the celebrated suite of furniture in the Picture Gallery.

Philip Mercier, the French artist whose chief patron was Frederick Prince of Wales, spent ten years in York from 1738, painting portraits of the local gentry. Although his style is generally characterised by a lively and informal Rococo quality some of his portraits are in the old fashioned full-length format. This suggests that his Yorkshire clientele were not entirely ready for his more cosmopolitan style and preferred their new portraits to blend with those of previous ages.

36 'Phillis, a Pointer of Lord Clermonts'

George Stubbs (1724-1806)

Oil on canvas 40 × 50 in (102.2 × 127.7 cm)
Signed and dated 1772 behind the hind legs,
and inscribed below the fore feet
Exhib and Lit: Jane Farrington, *Man's Best Friend*,
Birmingham Museum and Art Gallery 1991
Prov: Lord Forteviot; Henry Hutchinson; W R Rees –
Davies MP; bought from Leggatt Bros from the
Corporation Fund 1951 (£450)(14/51)

The pointer originated in 15TH century Italy and was used for hunting partridges. It hunts by scent, and when it detects hidden prey it freezes in its tracks, 'pointing' its head, with its neck stretched forward, its tail stretched horizontally, and its forepaw raised. In this portrait Phillis is about to 'point' and has an air of concentration in her face. She is an English pointer, the most popular breed at this time, greatly prized for its ability in hunting and retrieving.

Dogs were not usually given human names unless their master or mistress doted on them. This was a uniquely English custom, unknown elsewhere in Europe at this time. Obviously William Henry Fortescue, Lord Clermont, who was a keen sportsman and owned a substantial kennel, held Phillis in close affection.

George Stubbs, the greatest English sporting artist, had an unrivalled knowledge of anatomy which can be seen to great effect in his depiction of Phillis' posture.

37 Suffolk Landscape

Ebenezer Tull (1733-1762)

Oil on canvas 11 x 13 in (27.9 x 33 cm)
Lit: John Hayes, 'Ebenezer Tull, 'The British Ruysdale':
an identification and an attribution', *Burlington Magazine*
CXX no 901, April 1978, pp 232-3
Bought from the Harding Fund (as a Gainsborough) 1936
(£100) (29.2/36)

For many years this painting was thought to be an early work of the young Thomas Gainsborough, dating from his Suffolk period and before his move to Bath in 1759. However, an engraving of this scene in reverse, published by a leading art dealer of the day, named the artist as Ebenezer Tull.

Tull was a schoolmaster and amateur artist as well as a considerable collector of contemporary English and 17TH century Dutch landscape paintings. He specialised in 'Landskips' which were 'much in taste' at this time, especially when they imitated the earlier Dutch masters. After Tull's death the sale catalogue of his collection described him as 'the British Ruysdale'. On the evidence of this picture, the only firmly attributed work by this artist, he was greatly indebted to this master. He evidently had a neat touch, giving the foliage and foreground precise treatment and the sky a particularly subtle tone.

38 Portrait of Frances Maria Fountayne

Joseph Highmore (1692-1780)

Oil on canvas 50 × 40 in (127 × 101.6 cm)
Signed on plinth to left and inscribed *Frans. Maria Fountayne/Daughter of Thos. Whichcot Esqr.*
Bought from Mr R B Beckett from the Corporation Fund 1955 (£100) (25.4/55)

Frances Maria, daughter of Thomas Whichcote of Harpswell, was the second wife of Dr John Fountayne (1715-1802), Dean of York and owner of Melton Hall near Doncaster. Her husband was a close friend of the writer Lawrence Sterne, also a canon of York. She had one daughter, named after herself born in 1750. After her death her husband married Anne, daughter of Charles Montagu as his third wife.

Joseph Highmore achieved considerable popularity as a portrait painter of the gentry and professional classes because of his lively informal style in a francophile Rococo idiom learnt at the St Martin's Lane Academy. His illustrations from the best selling novel *Pamela*, by Samuel Richardson, were designed to be engraved and enjoyed a great success.

The portrait is one of a group of six of the Fountayne family of High Melton, near Doncaster, bought *en bloc* in 1955.

39 The Interior of the Pantheon, Oxford Road

William Hodges (1744-1797),
the figures by William Pars (1742-1784)

Oil on canvas 90¹/₄ × 120 in (228.8 × 304.8 cm)
Lit: William Wells, 'The Pantheon, Oxford Road',
Leeds Arts Calendar no 17 (1952), pp 11-20
Exhib: Grand Tour: the lure of Italy in the 18th century,
Tate Gallery, 1996-7 (253) (catalogue eds Andrew
Wilton and Ilaria Bignamini)
Prov: Wood family at Hickleton Hall (?); given the Rt Hon
the Earl of Halifax 1948 (22.108/48)

The Pantheon was one of the most spectacular sights of late 18TH century London. When it opened its doors as *the* venue for assemblies, concerts and social gatherings in 1772 it immediately established the reputation of its young architect James Wyatt. The lower part recalled Santa Sophia in Constantinople, while the dome (constructed of timber painted in *trompe l'oeil*) was obviously in imitation of the Pantheon in Rome. This inventive use of sources – never a blind copying of ancient prototypes – and interest in the 'movement' of architectural space (with different shaped areas, screens, and niches) was characteristic of early neo-Classicism in Britain. Here the colour schemes and furnishings (all designed by Wyatt) give a good impression of fashionable taste of the 1770s. The Pantheon burnt down in 1792 having been converted into an opera house.

William Hodges is best known for his work while accompanying Captain Cook on his second voyage of exploration 1772-5. He was also an accomplished architectural topographer and this picture is probably his most ambitious and successful example in the genre. The figures, according to a contemporary account, were painted by William Pars, an artist best known for his fine watercolours but who was also a registered portrait painter.

40 'The Fair Nun Unmasked'

Henry Morland (c1730-1797)

Oil on canvas 30 × 25 in (76.2 × 63.5 cm)
Lit: Helena Davis, 'The Fair Nun Unmasked',
Leeds Arts Calendar no 85 (1979), pp 5-10
Prov: Mrs Berryman; bought from Roland Browse and
Delbanco from the Corporation Fund (£375) 1948 (9.1/48)

This apparently ravishing evocation of 18TH century glamour conceals something rather more sinister. When it was first exhibited at the Free Society of Artists in 1769 it was simply entitled *'A Lady in a Masquerade Habit'*. Its more specific title *'The Fair Nun Unmasked'* appeared only after the picture had been engraved by the publisher Carrington Bowles some time later. The inscription which then appeared beneath the engraving was taken from Alexander Pope's famous poem *The Rape of the Lock*;

'On her white Breast a sparkling Cross she wore
Which Jews may kiss and Infidels adore'

In fact the picture shows a courtesan in masquerade costume, with her veil suggesting that she is a nun. Entertainments such as masquerades in which fancy dress took a major part were hugely popular especially with their potential for satire. Here the artist has chosen to mock the convention whereby ladies of easy virtue could employ the subterfuge of religious dress, including the use of devotional jewellery, to entice potential 'clients'. Thus the victim of this mild satire is the prostitute herself and the society which allowed her to use 'religion' as a smokescreen for vice. The description of a woman as a 'nun' in 18TH century Protestant England was to imply that she was a whore.

The identity of the 'Fair Nun' has long been the subject of speculation: names of celebrities such as Eva Garrick, wife of the great actor, or one of the Gunning sisters (the great beauties of the age, later Duchess of Hamilton and Countess of Coventry) have been suggested in the past. Henry Morland was the father of the more celebrated George Morland, the painter of rustic scenes.

41 Phaeton in a Thunderstorm

Julius Caesar Ibbetson (1759-1817)

(Also known as *Aberglaslyn: 'The Flash of Lightning'*)

Oil on canvas 26½ x 36½ in (67.3 x 92.7 cm)
Signed and dated 1798 bottom centre
Lit: Mary Rotha Clay, *Julius Caesar Ibbetson (1759-1817)*
p 36; Peter Webber, 'Catalogue of Paintings of Julius
Caesar Ibbetson at Temple Newsam May 1995',
Leeds Arts Calendar, no 116 (1995), p 21
Exhib and Lit: James Mitchell, *Julius Caesar Ibbetson
(1759-1817): 'The Berchem of England'*, John Mitchell
& Son 1999 pp 73, 97
Prov: Sir John Mildmay's sale Christie's 28 May 1914,
lot 128; bought from the Corporation Fund 1945
(£150) (5.1/45)

This melodramatic picture is based on a real event which took place during the artist's tour of Wales in 1792 in the company of the Hon Robert Fulke Greville (an equerry to the King) and a fellow artist John Raphael Smith. An inscription on the back reads: '*An actual scene. The Honble Robert Greville's Phaeton between Pont Aberglaslyn and Tan-y-Bwlch crossing the Mountain Range in a Thunder Storm. Painted by Julius Ibbetson who was the passenger*'. The artist has indeed painted himself as the figure placing a brake behind the wheel to ease the horses.

The earliest version of this scene appears to be a watercolour (now in the British Museum) which concentrates on the steep and narrow ascent of the road. This oil version, worked up several years after the event (1798), emphasises the dramatic elements of the storm itself, making particular use of contrasting light effects.

Julius Caesar Ibbetson was born in Leeds and became a talented landscape and genre artist travelling in search of the picturesque in the Lake District, Scotland, Wales and elsewhere before finally settling at Masham in Wensleydale. He also took part in an abortive expedition to Peking as an official artist. His art is often derivative of the Italian or Dutch masters but nevertheless he had a passion for nature and was intrigued by human oddities.

42 Portrait of a Young Man

Julius Caesar Ibbetson (1759-1817)

Oil on canvas 35¼ × 27½ in (90.2 × 70 cm)
Signed and dated 1790 bottom right
Lit: Mary Rotha Clay, *Julius Caesar Ibbetson (1759-1817),*
p 110; Peter Webber, 'Catalogue of Paintings of Julius
Caesar Ibbetson at Temple Newsam House May 1995',
Leeds Arts Calendar no 116 (1995), p 17
Exhib and Lit: James Mitchell, *Julius Caesar Ibbetson
(1759-1817): 'The Berchem of England'*, John Mitchell
& Son 1999, pp 64, 97
Prov: Mr Purdy; by 1869 Burdett-Coutts collection;
Baroness Burdett-Coutts sale Christie's 4 May 1922,
lot 39; bought from the Corporation Fund 1946
(£250) (8.1/46)

Although he considered himself primarily a landscape painter the Leeds-born Julius Caesar Ibbetson occasionally undertook portraits out of necessity 'to make the pot boil'. A small number, including this example, depict full length figures in a romantic landscape setting somewhat reminiscent of Thomas Gainsborough (who had died in 1788).

The Victorian tradition that the figure represents the poet Robert Burns cannot be sustained. Although Ibbetson and Burns were both the same age (thirty at the time of this painting) it is doubtful that they ever met although the artist later illustrated some of Burns' poems. The background here must refer to Wales since Ibbetson had not visited any other mountainous parts of Britain by this date. He was a guest of Lord Bute at Cardiff Castle in 1789 and so the figure may represent his patron's grandson John Stuart (1767-1794).

43 Conversation Picture
British School 18TH century

Oil on canvas 36 × 29 in (91.3 × 73.7 cm)
Bequeathed by James Rigby Esq 1940 (20/40)

A number of different artists have been suggested as the author of this well-known Conversation Picture: Benjamin Wilson, Henry Walton, Nathaniel Dance, David Allan – but none seems entirely convincing. 'Conversation Pictures' are a special genre of picture in which portraits of two or more figures are depicted informally in their everyday surroundings and often 'in conversation' with each other.

Despite its technical shortcomings (its poor perspective, the woodeness of the figures) the picture is remarkable for its depiction of a parlour belonging to a prosperous young couple of the mid 1770s. The fashionably dressed lady is shown 'knotting', or 'tatting' – making a decorative linen braid with the aid of a small shuttle which could be sewn onto fabric. This fashionable occupation, or 'work', had even become acceptable at Court and provided an excuse for ladies to show off the graceful attitudes of their hands. She is seated on an armchair with a 'Manchester check' case cover which is fastened with tapes.

On the floor is a lattice pattern 'ingrain' or 'Scotch' carpet with a border, fitted or 'planed' to the room. The window has a pair of 'drapery window curtains' which had superseded festoon curtains in popularity and which draw both horizontally and vertically at the same time. On the mantelpiece is a pair of griffin candlesticks probably made in Wedgwood's basalte-ware and first manufactured in 1771 after a design by the King's architect, Sir William Chambers. Between them *Flora*, goddess of flowers and the spring, appears to be giving the couple her blessing; she is a bronze-painted plaster reproduction made by John Cheere 'the man at Hyde Park Corner' (loosely based on the ancient version known as the Farnese Flora, but here holding a laurel wreath as though symbolisng Fame).

44 Portrait of William Pitt
Gainsborough Dupont (1754-1797)

Oil on canvas 30 × 25 in (76.2 × 63.5 cm)
Given by J G Uppleby 1858 (133/1858)

William Pitt the Younger (1759-1806) followed his father as the greatest statesman of his generation. He became Chancellor of the Exchequer at the age of 23 and Prime Minister at 24. He was responsible for a period of political stability following the turbulent years of the American War of Independence, and presided over the early military and naval successes following the outbreak of war against France in 1792. Despite his many qualities he seems to have been indifferent to the visual arts or literature.

When he sat to Thomas Gainsborough in 1787 for a portrait for the Duke of Buckingham the artist was struck by Pitt's 'hauteur and disrespectful manner'.

Gainsborough Dupont was the son of Thomas Gainsborough's sister. He was his uncle's only apprentice and assistant and finished a number of portraits left incomplete on the latter's death in 1788, including one of William Pitt. He must have painted a number of copies of his uncle's original of the statesman, but in 1796 he was commissioned to paint an entirely new full-length for Trinity House (subsequently destroyed). The Temple Newsam picture is a reduced version of this latter portrait, one of at least ten by Dupont.

45 The Return from Market
Francis Wheatley (1747-1801)

Oil on canvas 29¹/₂ × 24¹/₂ in (74.9 × 62.2 cm)
Initialled and dated 1786
Exhib: *Angels and Urchins: the Fancy Picture in 18th century British Art*, Nottingham University and Kenwood 1998 (88)
Prov: A McKay; Lord Northbrook; F J Nettlefold who presented it to Leeds 1948 (1.1/48)

Like Morland's '*The Fair Nun Unmasked*' (no 40), *The Return from Market* was engraved almost immediately after it had been painted. The enterprising publisher Charles Knight appended the following lines of verse referring to the esteem in which the innocent girl in the picture was held by her husband:

To him, more dear for what she never knew,
A prudent house-wife, virtuous, fond and true;
And lo! the pledge of truth, a rosy boy;
The father's opening form, the mother's joy.

The 'Fancy Picture', a genre generally dealing with moral subjects or extolling domestic virtue, had been developed by Hogarth and Mercier in the previous generation. Such pictures tended to lapse into a prettified sentimentality. Wheatley manages to avoid this in this example where his somewhat earthy, but pretty, young peasant woman is counting her day's takings from her stall at the market – '*an image of a happy hard working rural labourer, content with her lot in life and a credit to her family*'.

46 The Romps
William Redmore Bigg (1755-1828)

Oil on canvas 23½ x 28 (59.7 x 71.1 cm)
Exhib: Royal Academy 1795 (12)
Bought from the Corporation Fund from
Mrs W Roach 1954 (£160) (23/54)

The art of telling a story in paint culminated in the mid-19TH century with those realistic but sometimes sententious paintings of the 'every picture tells a story' type. This attractive example of the art of William Redmore Bigg, first exhibited in 1795, describes a trivial subject with a pleasing mixture of observation and humour. It was engraved by William Ward almost immediately after it was finished, as was its companion painting *The Truants Discovered* (private collection) in which a group of boys are being admonished by their gouty old tutor having stolen some pears.

The work of William Redmore Bigg was very popular in its day and he was a frequent exhibitor at the Royal Academy. His subjects were often moral ones, showing kind schoolboys, distressed sailors and the virtuous poor. The pictures were often made as pairs and were frequently engraved.

47 Portrait of Sir John Beckett

Sir Thomas Lawrence (1769-1830)

Oil on canvas 26 × 28 in (91.5 × 71.2 cm)
Lit: Kenneth Garlick, *Sir Thomas Lawrence* (1954) p 27
and revised edition (1989) p 148
Prov: the sitter's niece married Sir Hickman Bacon,
10th Bt; given by Sir Hickman Bacon 11th Bt 1934 (4/34)

The sitter (1775-1847) was a distinguished lawyer and head of the leading Leeds banking firm Beckett & Co who were responsible for developing much commercial activity in Leeds in the 19TH century. He was Judge Advocate-General for many years, and briefly MP for Leeds. In politics he was a strict Tory voting against parliamentary reform and many other liberal measures.

Sir Thomas Lawrence, President of the Royal Academy, was a hugely successful portrait painter who, at his best, could invest his sitters with grandeur and drama. In this portrait, painted towards the end of his life after 1820, he transforms a mundane banker into the image of a Byronic hero.

48 Portrait of Samuel Oldknow
Joseph Wright of Derby (1734-1797)

Oil on canvas 96 × 60 in (243.9 × 152.4 cm)
Exhib and Lit: Judy Egerton, *Wright of Derby*,
Tate Gallery, 1990 (128)
Prov: Mrs C J Pooley, from whom on long loan to Leeds
Art Gallery since 1900; bought from Lady Sutcliffe Smith
from the Corporation Fund 1950 (£40) (7/50)

Samuel Oldknow (1759-1828) of Stockport, Cheshire, rose to become the most successful manufacturer of fine muslins by the age of 30. His two fine mills contained the most up-to-date machinery including the spinning mule invented by Samuel Crompton and available from c1780.

Oldknow was known as a most humane and enlightened employer but ran into financial difficulties soon after the outbreak of the French wars in 1792. He had over-extended himself and was obliged to call in the assistance of the great industrialist Sir Richard Arkwright. Oldknow's portrait, painted about this time, cost 50 guineas and appears to have been paid for in instalments.

Probably the first pianoforte to be heard in the north of England was owned by Oldknow. It was despatched to him by his agent in London who wrote: *'I hope you will find sweet music in it that will wrap your soul as Milton says in Elizium'.* Wright has chosen to depict Oldknow with a bolt of fine muslin, the source of his wealth and success instead of the more conventional artistic or iconographic props.

50 Portrait of Mrs Brown, Housekeeper at Bramham Park
George Garrard (1760-1826)

Oil on canvas 18¼ x 14¼ in (46.3 x 35.6 cm)
Lit: James Lomax, 'A Glimpse Behind the Green Baize Door', *Country Life*, 22 October 1998, pp 104-105
Prov: Bramham Park; unknown US ownership; Christie's East, New York sale February 1997; bought 1998 with the aid of grants from the MGC/V&A Purchase Grant Fund, the Leeds Art Collections Fund, the Sir George Martin Trust, the Raymond Burton Charitable Trust, Leeds Decorative and Fine Art Society and the Brigadier Hargreaves Trust (£38,250 for the six)

This is one of a group of at least eleven portraits of servants painted in the early 1820s for George Lane Fox, the squire of Bramham Park, Yorkshire. Six of these are now at Temple Newsam, of which five were painted by George Garrard ARA and one by the Hull artist John Widdas. They have been identified as John Pollock the Steward, William Fox the Coachman, William Wright the Gatekeeper, a gardener and an elderly retired female domestic (smoking a pipe).

Mrs Brown the Housekeeper was the senior female domestic responsible for all the lower female servants and for the supervision of the kitchen, the laundry and the general housekeeping. She was unmarried (despite her honorific title of 'Mrs') and lived in the house. Together with the footman she was also responsible for locking up the house at night. She was still in service at the time of the fire which gutted the house in 1826. Garrard has painted her in the Dry Laundry after a tour of inspection, gazing out steadily from under her hooded eyelids with her arms folded as if satisfied with a job well done.

Servants' portraits are relatively rare and were usually undertaken by anonymous unskilled artists. The fact that most of the Bramham servants were painted by an Associate of the Royal Academy who was also undertaking portraits of the squire's family and animals is a testimony to the good relations which must have existed on either side of the green baize door at this time.

49 Portrait of William and Charles Chadwick
Charles Henry Schwanfelder (1774-1837)

Oil on canvas 40 x 34 in (101.6 x 86.4 cm)
Signed and dated 1824 bottom left
Lit: Adrian Budge, 'C H Schwanfelder – Animal Painter to The Prince Regent', *Leeds Arts Calendar*, no 85 (1979) pp 11-19; R Simon and A Smart, *The Art of Cricket* (1983), pp 103-4
Exhib: *The Fine Art of Cricket*, MCC 1997 (14)
Given by Miss Agnes Lupton 1936 (30/36)

William and Charles Chadwick came from a well-known family of prosperous Leeds dyers whose home, St Anne's Lodge at Burley, can be seen in the background. Charles later became chief physician of the Leeds General Infirmary and, together with the architect Sir George Gilbert Scott, was responsible for much of the planning of the new building which opened in 1868. In this picture the kneeling boy is presumably about to knock the stumps into the ground with the help of his cricket bat.

Schwanfelder was born in Leeds the son of a decorator of German origin. By 1800 he was advertising his skill as a 'painter and drawing master' in High Harrogate. He exhibited at the Royal Academy and at the first three exhibitions (1809-1811) organised by the Northern Society for the Encouragement of the Arts which attempted to encourage northern artists and patronage. He soon turned to other locations for his landscapes including the Lake District, Wales and Scotland. So successful were his animal pictures that in 1817 he obtained the Royal Warrant as 'Animal Painter to the Prince of Wales'.

Index